Amazing Girls
Around the World

Written by Sue Elias
Illustrated by Mithini Wathsala

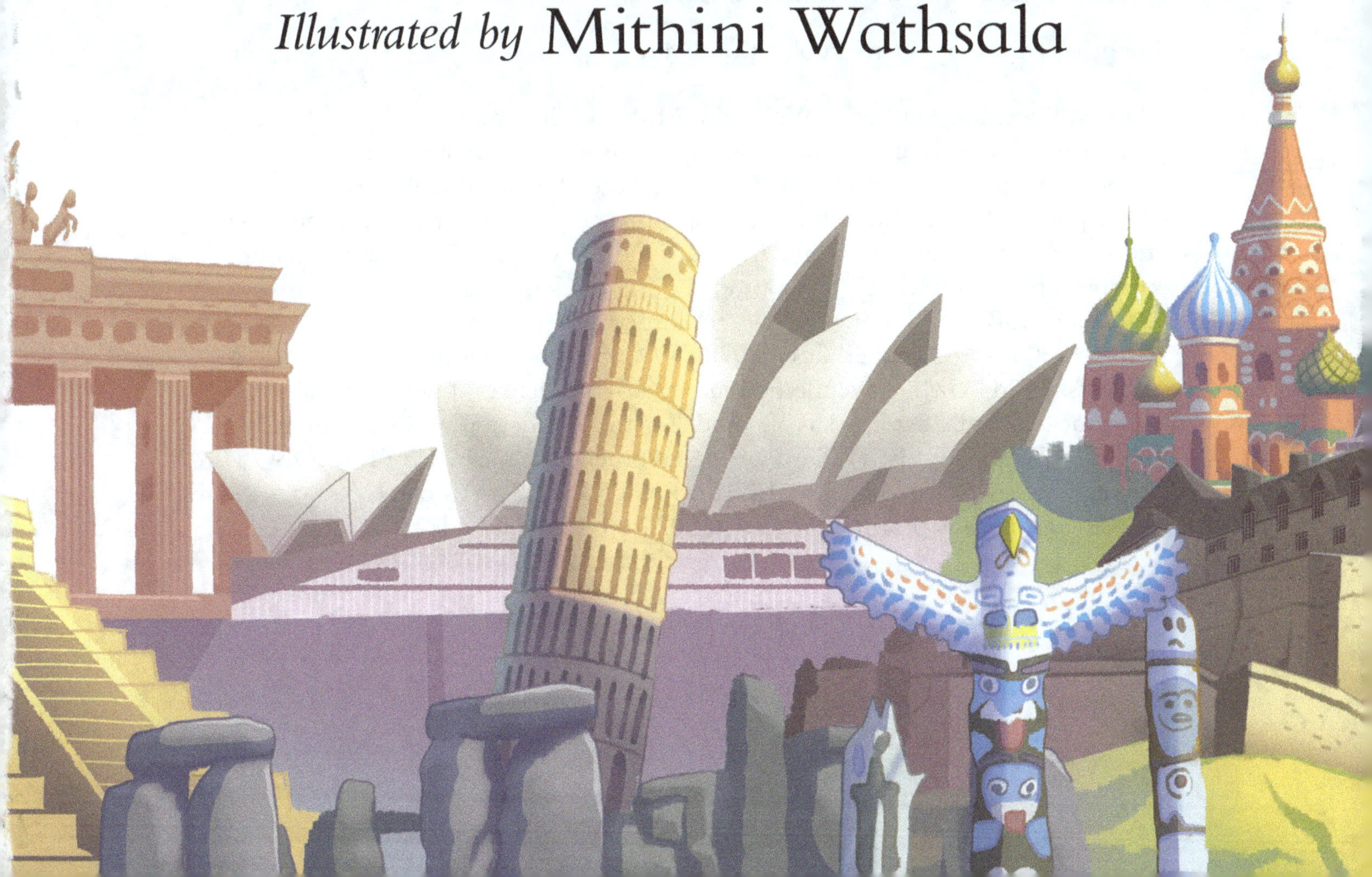

For information, permissions, or inquiries, please contact:

www.fairylandbooks.com

Cover Illustration by Remesh Ram
Interior Illustrations by Mithini Wathsala

Publisher's Cataloging-in-Publication Data

Names: Elias, Sue, author. | Wathsala, Mithini, illustrator.
Title: Amazing girls around the world : inspirational short stories for encouragement / written by Sue Elias; illustrated by Mithini Wathsala.
Description: Ontario: Sue Elias, 2025. | Summary: A collection of inspirational short stories about amazing girls from around the world, highlighting courage, kindness, and confidence to encourage young readers.
Identifiers: ISBN: 978-1-998058-68-6 (hardcover) | 978-1-998058-69-3 (paperback) | 978-1-998058-70-9 (ebook)
Subjects: LCSH Girls--Juvenile fiction. | Self-confidence--Juvenile fiction. | Courage--Juvenile fiction. | Role models--Juvenile fiction. | Short stories. | BISAC JUVENILE FICTION / Girls & Women | JUVENILE FICTION / Social Themes / General | JUVENILE FICTION / Short stories
Classification: LCC PZ7.1 .E4343 Am 2025 | DDC [Fic]--dc23

Contents

Dedication

To my precious granddaughter Noelle—
May these stories of amazing girls around
the world inspire you to follow your
dreams, trust your strength, and always
remember how truly extraordinary you are.

Introduction

Amazing Girls Around the World
To all the amazing girls—and the
dreamers who believe in them

All around the world, there are girls with big dreams, bright ideas, and kind hearts. Some live in quiet villages, others in busy cities, but all share a special gift— the courage to imagine, to care, and to make a difference.

In these twelve tales, you'll meet girls from every corner of the globe: from the green hills of Ireland and the misty castles of Scotland to the colorful festivals of Mexico and the golden beaches of Australia. You'll wander through Italy's art-filled streets, explore Canada's snowy towns, and dance to the rhythms of Brazil. Each story reveals a little magic, a lesson, and a spark of inspiration.

Each girl discovers her own special strength, kindness, creativity, courage, or determination—and learns that being amazing doesn't mean being perfect. It means believing in yourself, trying your best, and using your heart to make the world a brighter place.

As you read, you'll travel across continents, explore new cultures, and meet girls whose stories might remind you of your own. You might find courage in their bravery, hope in their dreams, or joy in their imagination.

So, find a cozy spot, open your heart, and let these stories take you on a journey around the world—one that celebrates how every girl, everywhere, is truly amazing.

With love,
The Author

*Confidence grows
when you believe
in yourself.*

Abigail and the Magical Pond

Abigail and her family lived in the English countryside in an old stone house that had been in their family for generations. She loved their garden, but she loved the surrounding forest even more. Deer and red squirrels were frequent visitors, and once in a while, Abigail would hear an owl—though she had never seen one.

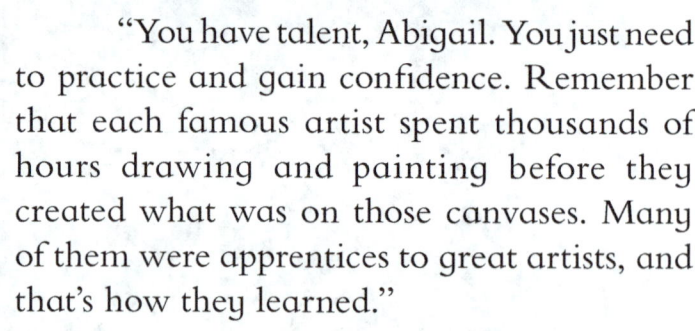

The beauty of the nature around her inspired Abigail, and she loved to draw. She would sit at a large wooden table with big sheets of white paper, crayons, or oil pastels. Sometimes she would start her drawing with colored pencils and then finish it with watercolors.

"Abigail, what are you drawing?" her mom asked one day.

"I'm trying to draw some of the beautiful flowers we have in our garden," Abigail said, "but my drawing isn't very good."

"I think it's absolutely beautiful," her mom replied. "The shapes of the flowers are correct, and the colors are gorgeous. Why do you think it isn't good?"

"You're not exactly objective, Mom. I'm your daughter, and you love me, so of course you're going to say it's beautiful."

Her mom smiled. "I wouldn't say your drawing was good if it wasn't."

"I just know that it could be so much better," Abigail lamented. "At school, when we go on field trips to art galleries or museums and see real art, I realize how much better I would have to be in order to become an acclaimed artist. I'll never be good enough. I don't have enough talent."

"You have talent, Abigail. You just need to practice and gain confidence. Remember that each famous artist spent thousands of hours drawing and painting before they created what was on those canvases. Many of them were apprentices to great artists, and that's how they learned."

"I think it would be so cool to learn alongside one of the great English painters, like Thomas Gainsborough or Margaret Sarah Carpenter," Abigail said. "We've been learning about these artists in school. They both painted portraits of their daughters."

"Just keep practicing. You'll get there," her mom said. "Why don't you take a walk outdoors? It's a beautiful day. You always seem to come back with fresh inspiration."

"Can I walk in the forest for a while?" Abigail asked.

"Yes, as long as you stay on the path," her mom agreed.

Abigail put her drawing things away and placed her binoculars around her neck. As she headed outdoors, the air was cool and there was a slight breeze. Wildflowers were blooming along the path, and Abigail stopped here and there to examine their colorful petals.

As she walked, she thought she heard the sound of an owl, but when she looked through her binoculars, all she could see were rustling leaves. She kept walking, and the owl's hoots grew louder and louder.

Then, suddenly, she saw the owl's enormous wings as it flew out of a treetop and over her head. It circled in the air above a small pond. Abigail was so excited to finally see the owl. It almost seemed as if the bird was sending her a magical message: *Stop here for a moment… stop here!*

She realized she had never noticed this pond on any of her earlier walks.

"I wonder if all the recent rains formed it," she thought.

She walked to the edge of the pond and looked into the clear water. All at once, ghostly shapes appeared. At first it was a bit frightening, but then the shapes became clear.

There was a young woman, standing at an easel, painting a forest scene. The painting looked exactly like the place where Abigail was standing at that moment. In the painting, a similar owl circled above a pond.

"How strange," Abigail whispered.

The young woman in the water's reflection hummed softly as she added the finishing touches to her painting. Abigail rubbed her eyes. She couldn't believe what she was seeing. She watched for a few minutes until the image of the young woman, and her painting began to fade.

On her way home, Abigail questioned what had happened. She wasn't sure she had truly seen the image. Perhaps she had imagined one of the famous painters of the past. That evening she searched online to see if she could find any painting like the one she had seen, but she found nothing.

Abigail didn't tell anyone. But every few days, after finishing her drawings, she returned to the pond. Each time, something exciting was happening.

She saw the young woman taking her paintings to different galleries. She saw her first gallery sale—the painting of the owl. She saw her own exhibition, filled with dozens of paintings, while art collectors praised her. She was invited to grand events in London.

Each time Abigail went home, she felt inspired to create more. She realized her mom had been right. Practice was making her work better and better.

One day, her older sister Olivia stopped and looked over her shoulder. "Abigail, your work is improving so much. Do you have a magical secret?"

"Yes," Abigail said with a smile. "I've been walking in the woods every day. Would you come with me today?"

"Sure… but aren't you going to tell me what it's all about?"

"No. You'll see when we get there," Abigail replied.

When the two sisters reached the pond, the owl circled overhead.

"Wow!" Olivia gasped. "That owl is so beautiful."

"It's just the beginning," Abigail said.

Both girls looked into the water as the surface began to shimmer. The scene formed slowly.

The young woman was older now. She walked into the Royal Academy of Arts in London, carrying brushes and paints. Soon she was teaching a class in oil painting.

Olivia gasped. "This is amazing. It's showing you in the future, Abigail! You're going to become a famous painter."

"Are you sure it's me?" Abigail asked. "I can't believe it. I never even noticed she looked like me."

"She even walks and talks like you. It's you for sure," Olivia insisted.

As they watched, the scene slowly evaporated.

When they returned to the pond a week later, all the water had dried up.

Abigail was sad, but she held the images of her future self in her heart. She forgot all about her lack of confidence. She

10

simply continued to practice and study.

A few months later, it was her birthday. Her parents and Olivia had special gifts for her.

Her dad announced, "Abigail, all of us have noticed how hard you're working on your art. We've started a special savings account for you so that by the time you're eighteen, you can apply to attend the Royal Academy of Arts in London. Thomas Gainsborough was one of its founders."

Abigail couldn't believe her ears. She was beyond excited. The scenes from the magical pond had given her a glimpse of what her future might be—and it was absolutely amazing.

The End

*When you care
for yourself,
you shine brighter.*

Barbara and the Self-Love Fairy

After a busy day at school, Barbara had just sat down to begin a new puzzle with a beautiful snowy landscape scene when her little brother, Bradley, came in.

"Barbara, are you busy?" Bradley asked. He was five years younger than Barbara, and he followed her around like a shadow.

Looking up from the puzzle piece she had just found, Barbara smiled at Bradley. She didn't really want to stop what she was doing, but instead, she said, "No…what is it?"

"I'm so bored…can we go outdoors and play in the snow?"

"Okay," Barbara said.

They both bundled up and went outdoors. It was the beginning of a very cold winter in Canada, and the snow was quite deep. Snowflakes had been falling for hours, leaving a powdery layer on top.

"Let's make snow angels!" Bradley exclaimed.

"Okay," Barbara said. She felt cold and didn't really want to, but she knew it would make Bradley happy.

After about an hour, they came back indoors with red cheeks. "Time for dinner and homework!" Mom exclaimed as she put a hearty stew on the table. Barbara thought to herself, *Now I won't have any time to work on my new puzzle.*

Barbara and Bradley's older sister, Jessica, came running into the dining room. "Sorry I'm late! I have a science project due this week, and I was trying to figure out what I'm going to do. I went to the library after school and lost track of time."

"That's okay, honey," Dad said. "Have you decided on your project?"

"Well," Jessica replied, "I was hoping that Barbara could help me after school tomorrow. She's so much better at science than I am."

Barbara said, "I'm supposed to have a playdate with my friend Emily tomorrow after school." She saw the disappointed look on Jessica's face.

"I guess I can reschedule. Emily will understand," Barbara added. "When did your teacher give you the assignment, and when does it have to be finished?"

"I think she gave it to us about a week ago, but it's due on Friday."

"This Friday?" Barbara asked. Jessica was always waiting until the last minute to get things done.

Jessica nodded.

After dinner, Barbara called Emily to reschedule. Emily sighed. "But this is the second time we've had to change it." Barbara could hear the disappointment in her friend's voice. *I just can't seem to make everyone happy no matter what I do,* she thought.

"I'm sorry, Emily. I'll make it up to you."

The next afternoon, Barbara spent three hours helping Jessica with her science project. She felt sad that she couldn't work on her new puzzle. She wished Jessica would be more responsible with her schoolwork. Jessica didn't love books and studying the way Barbara did, and she often depended on her younger sister.

The following day, the morning went by quickly, and Barbara was glad when it was lunchtime. Opening her lunchbox, she found an appetizing ham and cheese sandwich, some chips, a banana, and a chocolate chip cookie. She was starving.

Her friend Darla sat down next to her. "That looks yummy," she said. "Your mom packs the best lunches. I just have a peanut butter and jelly sandwich. I'm starving."

Barbara didn't say anything at first, but she could hear Darla's stomach growling like a tiny bear cub. "Here, Darla. Take my banana and cookie. I'm not that hungry today."

"Are you sure?" Darla asked.

"Yes," Barbara said, smiling. She ate her sandwich slowly and even offered some of her chips to Darla.

After lunch, it was time to go to the school library. When the library class was over, the students were allowed to check out books. Barbara searched for something different.

On a high shelf, she noticed a glittery cover. She pulled it down. The title was *The Self-Love Fairy.* She checked it out along with a couple of other books, but she didn't have time to read it until later.

At home before dinner, she tucked herself into the corner of her room with the book. Settling into her most comfortable chair, she propped it on her lap. She was tired and began to doze when suddenly she heard a tiny voice.

15

"Wake up, Barbara. It's important. I need to talk with you."

Startled, Barbara opened her eyes. A tiny fairy dressed all in pink was sitting on the open book pages.

"Who are you?" Barbara whispered.

"I'm the Self-Love Fairy, and I'm here to help you."

"What do you mean by self-love?" Barbara asked. She was so surprised it was hard to speak.

"Well...let me explain. You are a very kind person, Barbara, and that's a wonderful thing. BUT sometimes you need to set boundaries. You can't always sacrifice what you want just to make other people happy."

"I hate to disappoint people!"

"Yes, I understand," said the fairy, "but once in a while you need to put up a small invisible fence around yourself so others don't take advantage of you. Now, turn the pages of this book and watch yourself in these scenes."

The Self-Love Fairy flew off the page and perched on Barbara's shoulder while she turned the pages.

On the first page, she saw her brother Bradley asking her to play in the snow. Instead of saying yes right away, she told him she wanted to work on her puzzle for half an hour and then play with him for half an hour before dinner.

On the second page, she saw Jessica. In this scene, Barbara told her sister that she would help her brainstorm ideas, but Jessica would need to finish the project on her own. She also reminded her to ask for help sooner next time instead of waiting until the last minute. After all, her friends were important too, and she didn't want to disappoint Emily again.

On the third page, she saw Darla. Instead of giving Darla her banana and cookie, she shared them by splitting them in half.

When Barbara had seen herself in all the scenes, the Self-Love Fairy asked her, "Do you think you can try taking care of yourself a little better? I'd like to see you get to that new puzzle pretty soon."

Barbara nodded. "Yes, I'll try. Will you help me until I get the hang of it?"

"Yes," the Self-Love Fairy said. "You checked out this book for two weeks, and you can always renew it. And remember...boundaries are the space where you can love others and yourself at the same time."

Barbara smiled as the Self-Love Fairy flew back into the magical book. She knew the fairy was right. She needed to take better care of herself. It was important to love herself just as much as she loved everyone else.

The End

Kindness is the
truest power.

Delia Becomes a Leader

Delia and her family didn't own much, but they loved each other and were happy. One day, Delia's dad had an announcement for the family.

"I've lost my job. The factory is closing down, and it will be a while before I find another job to support us. Until then, your mom and I have decided that she will take you to your aunt's house in Louisville, Kentucky. Delia, you'll go to school there," he said.

Delia didn't say anything, but she felt very sad. She loved their home and her friends. Starting in a new school was always difficult. She looked across the dinner table at her younger brother John's face. He was upset they were moving too.

 A week later, Delia and John packed their few belongings and got into the truck. They said a tearful goodbye to their dad, and then their mom drove them away. They were all quiet for the better part of an hour. Delia watched as the landscape changed from small farmhouses to rows of two-story houses and crowded apartment buildings. They were moving to the city, and it was very different from their old neighborhood.

When they arrived, Aunt Cissy hugged and kissed them. "I'm so happy you're finally here!" she exclaimed. Delia had always liked and admired Aunt Cissy. She found her easy to confide in.

The next night after dinner, Aunt Cissy took Delia aside. "Are you excited about going to school here in Louisville?"

"I guess so," Delia said, "but I'm scared too."

"I understand," Aunt Cissy said. "I have something for you." She went to her jewelry case and took out a necklace. "I wore this when I was your age. I always believed it had magical powers. I'm giving it to you now, Delia, and I want you to wear it."

Delia looked closely at the necklace. The pendant was a star. She knew it wasn't real gold, but it made her feel special.

"Thank you, Aunt Cissy. I love it!" Delia exclaimed. She quickly put the necklace on and vowed never to take it off.

On the first day of school, Delia felt uncomfortable. She could tell she wasn't as well dressed as the other children in class. Her parents didn't have the money that the other kids' parents did. Her teachers did everything possible to make her feel welcome. A few students were friendly too, but most shunned her and made remarks about her clothes and her hairstyle.

A month passed. Delia was in the hallway when she noticed a boy putting up a poster. It announced that the student council was looking for a new president. Delia rubbed the magical necklace Aunt Cissy had given her between her fingers. She decided she wanted to be that new president.

At night at home, her mom and Aunt Cissy helped her create posters to hang around the school. Delia had received permission to put them up as part of her campaign. She was so excited. The idea of being a leader and helping to make the school better really appealed to her.

She placed the hand-lettered posters around the school and started working on her speech. She wanted to be clear about what she would do as president and how she would help her fellow students.

The next day, one of her friends stopped her in the hallway. "Delia, did you see your posters?" Ellen asked.

"No…what's wrong?" Delia replied.

"Carina did it. She's running for president too. She didn't think I saw her, but she used a marker and wrote awful things about you all over your posters."

"Like what?"

"Like she dresses like a farm girl, and she talks with a Southern twang."

"Those things are true, but they don't mean I can't be a good president," Delia said.

"I think you should go around and mark up her posters too," Ellen suggested.

Delia smiled. "I don't think it's a good idea for me to do that."

A few days later, it was time for Delia and Carina to make their presentations at the school. Word had spread, and everyone knew Carina had ruined Delia's posters. Delia stood in front of all the students. Despite her homespun dress, she had a commanding presence. The students were quiet and listened as she talked about the need for more tolerance and respect at school. Some nodded their heads, though Carina's friends sneered.

After Delia's presentation, she sat down in a chair on the stage.

Carina was ready to give her speech. She wore a beautiful dress with satin ribbons in her hair. Her polished new shoes gleamed. She carried her printed speech pages in her hand, smirking at Delia as she walked toward the stage. But suddenly she stumbled, and the pages flew everywhere. The audience gasped. For a moment, no one moved.

That's when Delia knew she should do the right thing. She jumped from her chair and helped Carina to her feet. She made sure Carina was okay, then gathered the scattered pages and handed them back in order.

Normally, the students would have laughed at Carina's fall. But seeing Delia's kindness toward someone who had tried to hurt her made them thoughtful.

Carina composed herself and began her speech. Much of it was about the school's image. She alluded to Delia's country clothes and her way of talking. Delia knew what Carina was trying to do, but she chose to rise above it. She wanted to be a true leader, win or lose.

That night, Delia told her mom and Aunt Cissy what had happened.

"I'm so proud of you, Delia," Aunt Cissy said. "You did the right thing. You are a star no matter who wins this election."

Her mom added, "I agree. You are brave, persistent, and kind—just like your father. I'm so proud of you."

The next day, the school posted the election results, and Delia had won by a wide margin. She couldn't wait to work with the student council. She was thrilled.

Carina passed her in the hallway. Delia could have ignored her, but instead she said, "Carina, would you like to be on one of the committees to plan social activities?"

"Really?" Carina asked. "I'd love that. I'm sorry for what I did."

"That's okay. You didn't say anything that isn't true. I do dress like a farm girl, and my voice does have a Southern twang," Delia said with a laugh.

"It was a mean thing to do," Carina admitted.

"Everyone does mean things once in a while," Delia replied. "But when we feel bad, we can always start again and do the right thing."

Both girls smiled at each other.

That night, Delia's dad called. He was excited—he had been invited to a job interview in Louisville. If he got the job, it might mean a better life for their family and a more permanent home close to Aunt Cissy. Delia was overjoyed. She couldn't wait to go to school in the morning. She had a feeling this was the beginning of a new life.

The End

*A little kindness makes
the biggest magic.*

The New Girl

It was the month of April, which in Australia is the middle of the autumn season. Cathy loved the colors of the leaves. Their bright red, gold, and orange hues made her feel happy. She also loved the sound of the leaves crunching under her feet as she walked to school. The walk to school was relatively short, just about a mile, and when the weather was beautiful, Cathy ate her breakfast quickly so she could spend more time enjoying it.

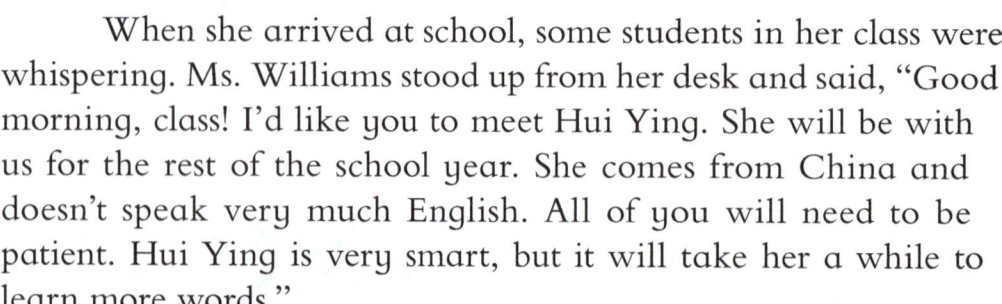

When she arrived at school, some students in her class were whispering. Ms. Williams stood up from her desk and said, "Good morning, class! I'd like you to meet Hui Ying. She will be with us for the rest of the school year. She comes from China and doesn't speak very much English. All of you will need to be patient. Hui Ying is very smart, but it will take her a while to learn more words."

Ms. Williams motioned for Hui Ying to stand so everyone could see her. Hui Ying rose and bowed slightly. She smiled a faint smile, and her cheeks turned pink with embarrassment. Cathy noticed Hui Ying's almond-shaped eyes and her long, black hair. She looked different from anyone else in class, and Cathy thought she was very pretty. Cathy smiled at her, but Hui Ying didn't notice.

English and science class went by quickly. Cathy glanced at Hui Ying and saw her studying the English textbook carefully. No one in class talked to her, even when Ms. Williams gave them free time to move around, ask questions, or work together. The others had paired off in groups, but no one sat with Hui Ying. Cathy was sitting with her close friend Evie. She thought about asking Hui Ying to join them, but she wasn't sure if Evie would be upset, so she stayed quiet.

During math class, Ms. Williams asked Hui Ying to go to the board and solve one of the assigned problems. It was a tough long-division question, and Hui Ying quickly worked it out—even though she wrote it differently than students in Australia did. "That's correct, Hui Ying! Good job!" Ms. Williams exclaimed.

Even though Hui Ying didn't fully understand what Ms. Williams had said, she recognized some of the words. From her teacher's tone, she knew she had done well.

Later that day, on the playground, Cathy noticed Hui Ying sitting alone on a bench. She couldn't tell if Hui Ying was sad, but her eyes glistened as though with tears. Maybe the cold breeze was stinging her face. Cathy wondered if Hui Ying was used to chilly weather in April.

Holding her soccer ball, Cathy walked up to her. With a few graceful hand gestures and simple words, she invited Hui Ying to play. Hui Ying understood and smiled. They laughed as they kicked the ball back and forth. When Ms. Williams noticed, she unfolded a goal post for them so they could practice making shots. "You're both doing great!" she said warmly. "I hope you're having fun."

Later that afternoon, when her mom picked her up from school, Cathy was unusually quiet. "Are you okay, sweetie? Were there any problems at school today?" her mom asked.

"I'm fine, Mom," Cathy said. "I'm just thinking. There's a new girl at school. Her name is Hui Ying, and she comes from China. She doesn't speak much English."

"That must be difficult. I can't imagine living somewhere without understanding what people were saying," her mom replied. "Does she seem nice?"

"Yes, she does. She's smart, and I like her smile. I played soccer with her today. Nobody else tries to talk with her or play with her," Cathy explained.

"I can understand that. A lot of patience is needed when you don't share the same language or culture," her mom said. "But I think I have something that may help you. When we get home, I'll give it to you."

After Cathy put her schoolbooks away, her mom came into her room carrying a small golden box. She placed it on Cathy's bed.

"What is this, Mom?" Cathy asked.

"Open it and you'll see," her mom said mysteriously.

Cathy opened the box. Inside was a stack of sturdy cards—not playing cards, but cards with pictures of everyday objects and actions. At the top of each card was a word or phrase in English, and at the bottom the same word or phrase was written in Chinese.

"Wow! Where did you get these, Mom?"

"We never talked about this, but when I was twenty years old, I went on a trip to China with a group from my college. Some of the students were from China, and I learned a lot about their culture, so I signed up to go. Of course, I didn't know any Chinese, so I thought these cards would help me. But I never anticipated what would happen when I started using them!"

"What happened?" Cathy asked, intrigued.

"I soon realized I could group the cards to form sentences or ideas when I communicated with someone. But there was more to it than that."

"What do you mean?" Cathy leaned closer, examining the cards.

"The more I used them, the more magical they became. Sometimes, when I couldn't figure out exactly what to say, I shuffled them, and a few cards would fall out. When I looked at the cards, I realized the deck had created a message for me."

"That's amazing! Do you think I could use them to talk with Hui Ying?"

"I don't see why not. I'm giving them to you, and I want you to promise to tell me what happens. There's one more thing—if Hui Ying can't find the exact words, she can use the cards too."

"This is so exciting! I'll bring them to school tomorrow. It's going to be fun!" Cathy exclaimed.

The next day, Cathy showed the cards to Ms. Williams and asked if it was okay to use them in class.

"These are amazing, Cathy. I've never seen anything like this. There are other students in our school who don't speak much English. I'll see if I can find card decks for their languages too. For now, it's fine for you to use them at recess and during breaks," Ms. Williams said.

At recess, Cathy showed the cards to Hui Ying. When Hui Ying saw them, a huge smile spread across her face. The two girls immediately began using the deck to communicate.

Within days, Cathy learned that Hui Ying had lived on a farm. The deck had pictures of many animals, and Hui Ying told Cathy her family had pigs, sheep, and chickens. She wanted to share more but couldn't find the right words. She shuffled the deck, and five cards fell out: Pig, Pen, Ran, Away, School. Then she pointed to herself.

Cathy thought for a moment. "Your pig got out of its pen, ran away, and followed you to school?"

Hui Ying nodded, and the two girls laughed and laughed.

A few months later, once Ms. Williams saw Hui Ying was more comfortable, she asked her to do a show-and-tell presentation. Hui Ying agreed if Cathy could help.

On the day of the presentation, the students asked Hui Ying about her life in China—where she had lived, what she liked to do, and whether she had siblings. They wanted to know what life was like in China and if she liked her new home in Australia.

Although Hui Ying was naturally shy, she happily answered. She told them what she liked to eat and explained how the seasons were opposite in China and Australia. The students were fascinated to hear that April in her hometown was springtime and much warmer. She also shared stories about her farm.

Ms. Williams took notes, planning to use the comparisons of cultures and seasons in future lessons.

Little by little, Hui Ying learned English. As the months passed, Cathy and Hui Ying grew close, using the magical cards to share their lives. Cathy even learned a few Chinese words. Hui Ying made other friends too, but Cathy became her best friend—because she had reached out before anyone else did.

The End

Hearts shine brighter
when they cheer
for others.

The Samba Performance

"Amanda, are you coming to dance class next Friday?" Ms. Santos asked.

"Yes! I'll be here, Ms. Santos. I hope we'll be practicing the samba," Amanda replied.

"Definitely! We'll be practicing the samba, the carimbó, and the bumba-meu-boi too," Ms. Santos said. "What about you, Carol? Will you be coming next Friday?"

"I'll be here," Carol said.

Carol and Amanda had been best friends since first grade, when Carol's family moved to Brazil. They shared many interests. They both loved reading books and were both good at science. At school, they often sat next to each other and shared lunch together.

Carol had never been very athletic, but Amanda loved dancing. In second grade, Carol went to watch Amanda's dance class. The beauty of the dancers and the rhythmic music delighted her. She could feel the drumbeats reverberating in her chest. The costumes were exciting too, with their shiny sequins and colorful feathers. Carol began taking lessons, and now that the girls were in fifth grade, this common interest had deepened their friendship even more.

One afternoon, both girls were at Carol's house. "I'd love to see the two of you perform," Carol's grandmother said. "If I put on some samba music, will you dance?"

"Sure!" Amanda exclaimed.

"Let's wear our feathered crowns so we look authentic," Carol suggested. "There's not enough time to change into our traditional dresses because Mom will have lunch ready soon."

Carol's grandmother put on a samba record. The sound was a bit scratchy, but it didn't matter. Carol and Amanda began to dance. Carol's grandmother clapped her hands as the girls swayed to the music.

Even Oro, Carol's green parrot, bobbed up and down on his perch as they danced.

As they moved, the delicious aroma of shrimp in coconut sauce drifted in from the kitchen, where Carol's mom was preparing lunch.

After about twenty minutes, Carol's mom said, "Okay, you two gorgeous dancers, it's time to catch your breath and sit down to eat." She then helped Carol's grandmother to the table.

Carol and Amanda served themselves fragrant white rice with spicy shrimp.

"Mom, this is delicious!" Carol said.

"I agree," Amanda added. "Thank you for inviting me."

"So, is your mom driving this week?" Carol's mom asked.

"Yes," Amanda said. "I think Ms. Santos is going to have us audition for the dance performance soon."

"What dance performance?" Carol asked.

"I overheard her talking to another teacher. She'll be auditioning us to see if we're good enough to dance with the older students," Amanda explained.

"That's very exciting!" exclaimed Carol's grandmother. "When I was young, I loved dancing the samba. I hope we'll be invited to watch the performance."

Soon Friday arrived. Amanda and her mom picked up Carol for dance class.

"Amanda, do you think Ms. Santos will start auditions today?" her mom asked.

"I don't know, Mom," Amanda replied. "I heard the teachers talking, but I didn't hear Ms. Santos say when we'd begin."

"Which part would you like to get?" Carol asked.

"There's always one girl who's the lead dancer," Amanda said. "That's the part I'd like."

"Uh oh…I wish I could be the lead dancer too," Carol admitted.

"We can both try out," Amanda said, "but probably one of the older, more experienced dancers will get it."

When they arrived at the dance studio, Ms. Santos announced, "Today each of you will audition for the lead role in the performance. If you're chosen, I'll be working with you for additional hours each week to prepare. The performance will be open to the public, so it must be polished before opening night."

The girls whispered nervously among themselves.

Ms. Santos continued, "I know it's nerve-racking to dance in front of your peers, but it's good practice. The real audience on performance night will be thousands of people. Carol, you'll perform the first samba."

Carol's stomach fluttered, but she was excited. She wanted the part. Ms. Santos started the music, and Carol began to dance. She tried to imagine no one was watching her.

When the five-minute dance ended, Ms. Santos said, "Excellent effort, Carol. You know the dance very well."

One by one, the other girls auditioned. Amanda was last.

"Okay, Amanda. It's your turn," Ms. Santos said.

Carol watched as Amanda stepped onto the stage. She was amazed at how graceful her friend looked. Amanda didn't seem nervous at all; her arms and legs moved fluidly with the rhythm. *She did better than I did,* Carol thought.

At the end of class, Ms. Santos said, "The teachers will meet over the next few days to decide. We'll call you if you get the lead. If we don't call, we hope you and your families will still be in the audience on performance night."

On Wednesday evening, Amanda called Carol. "Carol, I can't believe it! I got the lead part! I'll be the youngest dancer in the show. All the others are in the upper classes."

"That's fantastic," Carol said softly, though her heart sank. She had wanted it too.

"You sound a little strange," Amanda said. "Is everything okay?"

"Yes. But I have to go now. Let's talk later," Carol replied. She hung up and slumped in her chair.

That night at dinner, Carol was very quiet. Afterward, her grandmother said, "Come to my room and let's talk."

When they sat down together, her grandmother asked, "What happened today? You seem unhappy."

"Amanda called. She got the lead part in the samba performance. All the other parts went to older girls, so I won't be dancing with her," Carol said as tears filled her eyes.

"Isn't Amanda your best friend? I thought you'd be happy for her," her grandmother said gently.

"She is…I guess I'm just jealous because I wanted the lead," Carol admitted.

"I see," her grandmother said. "You know, Carol, life is full of choices. The things you want when you're young will change as you grow older. I once had a best friend like Amanda, but she moved away ten years ago. Now tell me—what's more important to you, getting the lead part or keeping Amanda as your friend?"

Carol paused. "I'm sad I didn't get the lead, but my friendship with Amanda is more important to me."

"Good," her grandmother said. "Then open your heart and be happy for her. Let your jealousy vanish like a puff of dark smoke. I have something special for you. It's magical, and I want you to have it."

Her grandmother rose slowly and went to her dresser. She returned with a large pink feather. "This is from the last samba costume I wore. It's yours now. When you wear it, remember that life is short. Be happy and dance as much as you can. Someday you'll be old like me and only able to dance in your imagination. Love your friends and love your life. Push away sad thoughts like jealousy. Your time to shine will come, but for now, be happy for Amanda."

Carol smiled. She knew her grandmother was wise. She took the beautiful feather and decided she would wear it on the night of the performance—happy and proud of her best friend.

The End

*Be proud of what
makes you unique.*

Charlotte's Hobby

Charlotte loved shiny things. She collected buttons, rocks, sequins, and anything else that sparkled. When she was six years old, her mom gave her a sparkly button—a blue one with tiny rhinestone glints—and Charlotte loved it. It became the first item in her collection. Her mom gave her empty egg cartons, and she placed her treasures inside. She often rearranged them by color, by sparkle, or by size.

Each rock, button, and glittering object had a story behind it. On a nature walk with her dad, she found a shiny piece of quartz and brought it home. When her grandmother sewed new buttons on a coat, she gave the old sparkly ones to Charlotte. Her brother, William, sometimes brought home a shimmering rock from geology class. Charlotte tucked them all into her egg cartons and remembered every story.

Now and then she added shells. Her family took her to Dog's Bay near Galway, where they lived. Charlotte loved the sea air and exploring the shoreline. The blue mussel shells were her favorite; their insides gleamed like iridescent pearls.

Every year the family drove to Adrigole Harbour, and during the five-hour trip her grandfather told stories. One favorite was about the shiny white fairy rock.

As they neared the harbour, Charlotte spotted the white fairy rock about two-thirds of the way up the hill above the water. But as they got closer, it looked as if the rock had moved—now it sat at the very top of the hill, white and gleaming for everyone to see!

"How did it get there? We just saw it farther down," Charlotte asked, astonished.

"Well, why do you think it's called a fairy rock?" her grandfather replied.

"I guess the fairies lifted it into the air and carried it up!" Charlotte exclaimed. "I wish I could have seen their magic."

"Me too," he said. "I'm sure they did it while we weren't looking. They like to play tricks on travelers."

"Are there other magical rocks up there?" Charlotte asked.

"I've heard there's a big one that opens a door to another world."

"Then fairies and elves and leprechauns must live there. Do you think we could explore and find it?"

"Maybe when you're older—and before I'm too old," he said with a grin. "It's a steep climb."

"Okay," Charlotte said. "Maybe when I'm ten. I think I could climb it then."

"I'll try to stay young enough to go with you," her grandfather promised.

The next year, after their trip to Adrigole Harbour, Charlotte turned eight. On her birthday, her parents asked if she'd like to go to summer camp. "Yes! Can my best friend, Erin, go too?" she asked.

"We'll talk to her parents," her mom said.

Erin's parents agreed, and a few days later the girls were packed and ready. Charlotte's mom drove them to camp. Both girls were buzzing with excitement.

"Be safe, and don't go exploring without a counselor nearby," Charlotte's mom reminded them at drop-off.

"Don't worry, Mom. Erin and I will be careful," Charlotte said, leaning in to kiss her goodbye.

In the meeting hall, a counselor, Ms. Britton, welcomed everyone. "We have lots of optional activities: sports and games, volleyball, soccer, archery, swimming in the lake, and nature walks on approved trails. You're here to relax, have fun, and make new friends."

Charlotte raised her hand. "Can I go exploring and collect rocks? My mum said not to go without a counselor close by."

Some girls giggled.

"Yes, that's fine," Ms. Britton said. "Always walk with a friend and stay on the marked trails. Counselors are often out there too. You might see a fox or other woodland creature, but there aren't any bears, coyotes, or snakes in Ireland."

"Okay," Charlotte said, puzzled by the giggles.

After the meeting, she asked Erin, "Why were they laughing at me?"

"I'm not sure. Maybe because you said you collect rocks," Erin said.

"Why is that funny? It's my hobby and I love it."

"I think it's cool," Erin said. "But you know how kids can be. They don't get what they haven't tried."

The next day a group of girls gathered for soccer. They asked Charlotte and Erin to join.

"I'll play for a while," Erin said.

"Thanks, but I want to explore and look for rocks," Charlotte replied.

Greta, the most athletic girl, scoffed. "Why would anyone collect rocks? That's a silly hobby."

Greta's best friend, Eva, added, "Yeah. What's so interesting about rocks?"

Before Charlotte could answer, the girls—and both soccer teams—trotted off. Erin waved goodbye and went with them.

Charlotte felt a pinch of sadness that Erin hadn't stayed, but she understood.

She decided to ask Ms. Britton for a trail map. In the meeting room, Ms. Britton was posting the day's activities.

"Ms. Britton, is there a map of the trails? I'd like to look for rocks for my collection," Charlotte said.

"Yes, I have one—but you can't go alone. Isn't Erin going?"

"She went to play soccer."

"I see. Well, I have a free hour," Ms. Britton said. "I can walk with you if you'd like. I love rocks. I had a collection when I was your age, and I still keep some in my garden."

"I'd love that," Charlotte said with a bright smile.

They headed down the first trail, a lovely path lined with trees and wildflowers. Now and then Charlotte picked up a shiny stone and slipped it into her backpack.

After a while, Charlotte noticed something unusual in a field on the right. At first it looked like a ring of stones. "What's that?" she asked.

"It's a fairy ring—mushrooms growing in a circle," Ms. Britton said. "Legend says fairies dance there at night or at dawn to make their magic."

"That's so cool," Charlotte said. "I wish I could see them."

"I'll tell you a secret. I think I saw one once," Ms. Britton whispered. "She wore a pink, shimmery dress and was about the size of my hand. I never told anyone. It was a couple of years ago."

"Why didn't you tell?" Charlotte asked, delighted.

"People sometimes mock what they haven't experienced," Ms. Britton said.

"Yes. Some girls make fun of me for collecting rocks," Charlotte said. "But it's my hobby, and I'm not going to stop."

"That's brave, Charlotte," Ms. Britton said. "If I organize an activity where everyone shares hobbies, will you talk about your rock collection?"

"Sure. It hurts when they laugh, but this is my passion."

The following week, Ms. Britton hosted the sharing circle.

Greta went first, talking about soccer. Everyone listened and clapped.

Eva shared her love of soccer and archery. Everyone listened and clapped.

One by one the campers spoke, and everyone listened.

Erin talked about the sports she liked and the baking she did with her mom.

Finally, it was Charlotte's turn. Except for Erin, some girls giggled as she stood. Charlotte's cheeks turned a bit pink, but when she began talking about her collection and why she loved it, everyone got quiet. She explained how each rock held a memory. She described the blue mussel shells from Dog's Bay and told the story of the fairy rock at Adrigole Harbour. A few girls giggled again at the mention of fairies.

Then Ms. Britton interrupted. She shared the story of when she saw the pink fairy and she told everyone about the fairy ring that she and Charlotte had seen on the trail. She even shared the fact that she had rocks in her garden that she had collected when she was a girl.

Later that day, Greta and Eva approached Charlotte. "We're sorry we made fun of you," Greta said. "We get why you love your hobby now. Could we explore with you sometime?"

"Sure," Charlotte said, smiling.

The next day at lunch, Erin said, "I loved your stories yesterday. And I thought it was great that Ms. Britton walked with you when I went to play soccer. I'll go with you next time."

"That would be great," Charlotte said.

That night the girls sat in a circle around the campfire. Ms. Britton stopped by to talk with Charlotte. "I admire you," she said. "Your courage helped me be brave too. Students learn from teachers, but teachers learn from students as well."

Charlotte felt happy. Looking around at the circle of girls talking and smiling, she thought, *we've made a fairy ring of our own.*

The End

Courage can turn
fear into strength.

The Empathy Ring

Jeanne and her class in Mexico City were getting ready for the Day of the Dead parade. Jeanne was part of the prestigious color guard for her school, and she had been practicing her marching steps and graceful flag twirls for weeks. Because she was a good student, she had quickly been nominated to represent her classmates.

Jeanne had many friends, including a boy named Arturo. He was smart and kind, but shorter than most boys his age. One day, Jeanne noticed a taller boy shoving Arturo in the hallway. The boy called him names and snatched things from his locker. Jeanne didn't interfere, but later at recess, when she had a quiet moment alone with Arturo, she asked him about it.

"Arturo, who was that boy, and why was he pushing you?" Jeanne asked.

"His name is Santiago," Arturo said. "He wanted me to give him answers to an exam. I refused, so now he's bullying me because I'm short."

"I think we should tell our teacher," Jeanne said.

"No, please don't," Arturo pleaded. "He lives in my neighborhood. If he finds out, he'll bother me day and night. I'm trying to ignore him, so he'll eventually stop."

"Okay," Jeanne agreed. "I won't do anything without your permission, but I'm worried he might hurt you."

"Don't worry. I know you're my friend and you care about me, but I'll be fine."

Still, Jeanne was troubled as they went back to class. Santiago lingered in the hallway, glaring at them. She could tell Arturo was afraid.

That afternoon, Jeanne's mom picked her up. "Let's buy some pan de muertos," her mom suggested.

"That sounds delicious," Jeanne said. She loved the sugary bread that filled bakeries before the Day of the Dead.

"We'll make hot chocolate too," her mom added.

Jeanne was thoughtful. "Mom, do you think our ancestors would be proud of us?"

"We all make mistakes, but I know one thing: our ancestors would be proud of you," her mom exclaimed.

"Thanks, Mom. I hope so, but sometimes I don't know how to help when I see a problem I didn't cause."

"What do you mean, honey?"

"Well, do you remember my friend Arturo?"

"Yes, I met him and his parents once. Is he okay?"

"He has a problem. A boy at school wanted him to cheat on an exam. Arturo said no, but now this boy, Santiago, is bullying him for being short."

"Did you try to help?"

"No. I thought it might make things worse. I wasn't sure what to do."

"Did you think about telling your teacher or the principal?"

"Yes, but Arturo asked me not to. Santiago lives in his neighborhood, so he's afraid he'll get in more trouble if we do."

Her mom sighed. "I see Arturo's point. After dinner, talk to your abuela. She is wise. She'll know what to do."

Jeanne's abuela, almost ninety, lived in a little cottage in their backyard. Jeanne often visited her after dinner. The cottage was filled with fascinating objects, each with its own story.

That night, her abuela wasn't feeling well, so Jeanne's mom asked her to bring over pozole rojo and some pan de muertos. Jeanne set the dishes on the table.

"Yum!" her grandmother said. "My arms ache. Would you feed me a few spoonfuls?"

"Of course," Jeanne said, carefully feeding her.

"You have a problem you want to discuss, don't you?" her grandmother asked.

"Yes! How did you know?" Jeanne gasped.

"Grandmothers always know."

Jeanne told her the whole story. Her abuela listened and nodded.

"Go to the top drawer of the dresser and bring me the black box inside."

Jeanne opened the drawer, found the box, and felt a surge of energy as she lifted it.

"Open it," her abuela said.

Inside was a ring with a red stone. "It's beautiful," Jeanne whispered.

"It's powerful," her grandmother said. "It's an empathy ring, passed down for generations. Here's what to do: wear it to school tomorrow and let Santiago notice it. He'll want it. Refuse at first, but when he insists, give it to him. Once he wears it, he'll never bully Arturo again. I promise."

The next day, Jeanne followed her instructions. She toyed with the ring until Santiago noticed.

"That's a boy's ring, not a girl's. Give it to me," he demanded.

"No, it's mine," Jeanne replied, spinning it on her finger.

"I'll take it if you don't hand it over," Santiago snarled.

Pretending to resist, Jeanne finally gave him the ring.

As soon as Santiago slipped it on, he staggered and sank onto a bench. His hand clutched his chest as waves of emotion crashed over him. For the first time, he felt everything Arturo had felt—the pain, fear, and humiliation of being bullied.

"What did this ring do to me?" he wailed. He yanked it off and dropped it. Jeanne quickly retrieved it and slipped it into her pocket.

Arturo, seeing them, hurried over. "Santiago, are you okay?"

"Why do you care how I feel?" Santiago asked hoarsely. "I've always been mean to you."

"I don't want anyone to suffer," Arturo said gently, "even someone who hurt me."

Tears welled in Santiago's eyes. "I won't do it again. Now I know how you felt."

That evening, Jeanne visited her abuela again.

"What happened?" her grandmother asked.

"I'm not completely sure, but I think Santiago felt Arturo's emotions. He was overwhelmed."

"Yes," her abuela nodded. "That's exactly it. Empathy is a learned skill. Santiago had never been able to imagine others' pain. Thanks to the ring, he is changed forever."

"Thank you so much!" Jeanne exclaimed. "I'm glad Arturo won't be bullied anymore."

"Me too," her abuela said warmly. "I'm proud of you, Jeanne. You protect others with kindness."

Jeanne blushed. "I almost forgot—here's the ring."

"Put it back in the box for me," her grandmother said. "Then let's have more pozole rojo. I want to get better so I can watch you perform in the parade."

"I hope you can," Jeanne said, hugging her. "That would be wonderful."

The End

The heart shines
brightest when it gives.

Theresa's Special Valentine

Theresa loved to draw and paint. At her home in Rome, she often sketched her family, her dog, and her cat. Her mom would say, "Theresa, this picture is beautiful! I'm putting it on the refrigerator. Someday you'll be as famous as Leonardo da Vinci or Michelangelo!" Theresa blushed at her mom's praise, but it made her feel good to have her talent encouraged.

At school, her teacher, Ms. Buongiorno, set aside an hour each afternoon for drawing or arts and crafts. It was Theresa's favorite time of day.

One Wednesday in mid-January, Ms. Buongiorno announced, "Valentine's Day is only a few weeks away. I'll have boxes of *baci perugina* for each of you." Theresa loved those traditional hazelnut-filled chocolates with their tiny love quotes tucked inside. Whenever she got a box, she always shared it with her family.

Her teacher continued, "You may use art time each afternoon to make valentines for your classmates. You'll have crayons, pastels, watercolors, acrylic paints, scissors, construction paper, and colorful glitter. Just be careful not to get the glitter all over the floor!"

Theresa wanted to make special valentines for her five closest friends—Eva, Angela, Gloria, Maria, and Celeste. First, she needed to ask them questions without revealing her plan.

Early in the week, she stopped Eva in the hallway. "Eva, what's your favorite color?"

"Purple," Eva replied. "What's yours?"

"Bright red—the color of Valentine's Day," Theresa said with a grin.

"Why do you ask?" Eva wondered.

"No special reason," Theresa answered, hiding a smile. She was already imagining Eva's valentine.

Throughout the week, she learned the others' favorite colors: Angela liked pink, Gloria liked teal, Maria liked blue, and Celeste liked green. Theresa already knew their pets or favorite animals, so she planned to draw them on each valentine.

During art class, Theresa began Eva's valentine. Since her friends sat nearby, she left the names and messages off for now. As she glued purple glitter around a heart-shaped card, Ms. Buongiorno walked by.

"That valentine is beautiful, Theresa. Who is it for?"

"It's a secret," Theresa whispered, smiling.

"Well, whoever gets it will be very happy," Ms. Buongiorno said warmly.

A few days later, Theresa worked on Angela's valentine. Angela happened to sit beside her. Glancing over, she admired it. "That one with the pink glitter is so pretty. Who's it for?"

"It's a secret," Theresa replied, covering her mouth to hide her smile.

Little by little, Theresa finished all five valentines. She was so excited she could hardly wait for Valentine's Day.

The night before, the family gathered for dinner—her parents, her brother Alfie, and her grandmother, Nonna. They ate lasagna her mom had baked, along with fresh bread and salad. The aroma of tomato sauce and ricotta filled the house.

"What's that on your fingers, Theresa?" Nonna asked.

Theresa laughed. "Paint stains. I've been making valentines for my friends."

"I hope you get lots in return," Nonna said.

Theresa nodded. "I can't wait. And Ms. Buongiorno promised us *baci perugina* too."

"I love those special chocolate kisses," Nonna said, licking her lips. "Will you save me one?"

"Of course! I'll save the whole box," Theresa said, blowing her grandmother a kiss.

The next day, Valentine's Day, Ms. Buongiorno announced, "We'll play games, eat cupcakes, and exchange valentines. Everyone, please give me your cards, and I'll distribute them later."

Theresa handed in her valentines, including one she had made for her teacher.

Just then, Filomena slipped in late. She was quiet, shy, and almost never spoke in class. Today her eyes were red, as if she had been crying. Ms. Buongiorno bent down and whispered to her, but Theresa couldn't hear what was said.

By the end of the day, Ms. Buongiorno handed each student a heart-shaped folder. She had written a valentine for every child, though most only received one or two from classmates. When Theresa opened her folder, she found just three—one from Eva, one from Celeste, and one from her teacher. She felt disappointed. Then she noticed Filomena. Her folder contained only Ms. Buongiorno's card. No valentines from friends.

That evening, Theresa sorted through her valentines. Though pretty, they weren't nearly as special as the ones she had made. She sighed.

Noticing her mood, Nonna said, "Come to my room, child."

Theresa followed her into the cozy room and sat across from her in a chair.

"What's the matter, Theresa?" Nonna asked gently.

"I worked so hard on valentines for my five best friends," Theresa admitted. "But I only got two back, plus the one everyone got from Ms. Buongiorno."

"I see," Nonna said. "But did you bring me my special chocolate kiss?"

Theresa smiled faintly. "Yes, I forgot. It's in my room." She returned with the box and handed it to her grandmother.

"Thank you," Nonna said, unwrapping one. She read the slip aloud: "*A gift given in secret is worth two.*" She looked up. "That's true, and I have a secret gift for you."

From her pocket, she drew out a small gold charm.

"What is it?" Theresa asked.

"A magical heart charm for your bracelet," Nonna explained. "Whenever you're sad, rub it. It may whisper an idea that brings you happiness."

Theresa examined it. One side was etched with the word *grateful*; the other read, *Helping one person may not change the world, but it could change the world for one person.* She rubbed the charm, and already she felt lighter.

"Thank you, Nonna," Theresa said, kissing her cheek.

Back in her room, she added the charm to her bracelet. The gold heart gleamed among the silver ones. Sitting at her art table, she suddenly knew what to do. It was as if a voice in her heart was guiding her. She created a valentine more beautiful than any before and wrote, *Filomena, will you be my friend? Love, Theresa.*

The next morning, she quietly left the envelope on Filomena's desk.

Later, as Theresa's friends gathered to thank her for their valentines, she thanked Eva and Celeste for theirs. She rubbed her charm and realized she no longer felt disappointed. She was grateful for the friends she had.

Then Filomena walked in. She noticed the envelope, opened it, and her face lit with a smile as her eyes filled with happy tears. She turned and looked at Theresa.

At that moment, Theresa knew the heart charm's magic had worked. She had given Filomena joy when she needed it most—and in doing so, had found happiness herself.

The End

*Friendship begins
with a simple hello.*

Cookies for Mrs. Novikov

Gloria and her family lived in a small country town in Russia called Staritsa. The schoolhouse was not far from her house in an old stone building. Gloria walked there every day. As she was walking, sometimes one or two of her friends would come out at the same time and they would walk together.

Her friend Maxim lived right next door, so he was the first to join her.

"Hello, Gloria! How are you?" Maxim asked as he bounded out of his front door.

"I'm good," Gloria said. "Have you finished your assignment?"

"Yes," Maxim said. "I am ready for the teacher to ask me any questions."

"I think I'm ready too."

They had walked a few blocks before they passed by the old woman's house. They passed by this house every day, but Gloria had never seen the old woman. There was talk of her in the town and everyone seemed to be afraid of her, but Gloria didn't know exactly why. Thorny vines covered the house and pieces of its stone facade were crumbling. No one had cleaned the outside of it for many years.

She thought she had seen the old woman peering out of the black curtains on the second floor once, but she wasn't certain because a second later her face wasn't there anymore.

Everyone in their school called the old woman Baba Yaga after the traditional fairy tale Russian witch who lived in a hut in the woods. No one knew her real name.

"I'm glad you are walking with me," Gloria said. "I don't like walking past that house by myself."

"I don't like to pass it either," Maxim said. "It's kind of eerie."

After another half block, their friend Sasha stepped outside of her house and joined them.

"How are both of you?" Sasha asked.

"We survived walking past Baba Yaga's house," Maxim said.

"Ivan said she captures children like in the fairy tale," Sasha said.

"That's not possible! The police would come to get her. Ivan is always making up stories," Gloria said. "You can't believe him."

"I don't know," Maxim said. "Everyone is scared of her. There must be a reason."

After school was over that day, Maxim and Sasha had to go to band practice so Gloria had to walk on her own. As she walked by the old woman's house, she noticed that there were thorny vines started to grow around the front door.

When she got home, her mother was gathering some ingredients in the kitchen.

"What are you doing, Mama?" Gloria asked.

"I'm going to make some tea cakes and some pryaniki," she replied. "Would you like to help me?"

"Yes!" exclaimed Gloria. She loved these traditional cookies. She couldn't determine which ones were her favorites. The tea cakes were nutty on the inside and rolled in powdered sugar and the pryaniki were made with honey combined with cardamom, ginger, and mace. The cookies were filled with plum or apricot jam, and they smelled so enticing. Gloria's mouth was watering as she thought about biting into one.

As they started the baking, Gloria told her mother about her day at school. Then she told her about Baba Yaga and what the other children had said about her. "Do you know her real name, Mama?" Gloria asked. "Is she really a witch?"

"Of course not! She just has a scary, wrinkled face. Her name is Mrs. Novikov," Gloria's mama said. "I heard a rumor that when she was young she was a ballerina, but I don't know if that is true. Other than that I know nothing about her, but I'm sure she is not a witch! She is just an old, lonely woman. Her husband died ten years ago."

"Why are those thorny vines all around her house?" Gloria asked.

"I don't know. When people get old sometimes they can't take care of things the way they used to when they were younger. Maybe she has no one who can help her."

"Ivan said that she's a witch like Baba Yaga and she captures children."

"What a ridiculous thing to say! Ivan makes up stories. You should never listen to him. When we are done baking these cookies maybe you can take some to Mrs. Novikov and meet her yourself. Then you will see that there is nothing to be afraid of."

"I couldn't do that," Gloria said. "I would be way too scared."

"Sometimes it is important to face your fears. Besides I will give you something special to take with

57

you. It is a magical cloth that will protect you. If you carry it with you, no one can harm you," her mother said. "But I'm absolutely sure that Mrs. Novikov will be very nice to you otherwise I would not let you go there. She probably never has visitors."

"Okay," Gloria said, but she was still very scared.

The next day was Saturday and Gloria's mama prepared a beautiful basket of cookies for Gloria to bring to Mrs. Novikov. Then she handed Gloria the special cloth.

"This is a Stenovoi plat," Gloria's mama said. "It's magical."

Gloria looked at the cloth. It had a crosshatch red pattern and tassels. "Did you embroider it, Mama?" she asked.

"Yes, my mother helped me do the embroidery when I was very young."

"It looks like a towel," Gloria said. "Do I wipe my hands with it?"

"No! You can wear it for protection, but it isn't like a dishtowel. Sometimes people hang it on their walls to protect their homes."

Gloria took the Stenovoi plat and draped it over one arm. Then she took the basket of cookies and draped it over her other arm.

Gloria tried to be brave as she walked out of the house. She was actually walking very, very slowly because she didn't really want to get there.

When she arrived, she opened the gate. It creaked as she opened it. The front yard was a mess and when she got up to the front door she couldn't find the doorbell. It was hidden by some of the vines. She gently pushed the vines aside and found it. She rang the doorbell, but no one came to the door. She waited for a few minutes, but she was wondering how long she should stand there before she turned around to go home.

Then she heard footsteps slowly going down the stairs and then coming up to the front door. Mrs. Novikov opened the door just slightly as if she were scared to open it wide. "Hello," she said in a timid voice that was almost a whisper.

"Hello, Mrs. Novikov," Gloria said. Her voice cracked slightly because she was still a little scared. "My name is Gloria. My mama and I baked some cookies for you."

Mrs. Novikov looked down at the cookies and a small smile spread across her wrinkled face. She didn't say anything, but tears filled her eyes. "Please come in, Gloria. I will fix some tea, and we will have cookies together."

Gloria didn't want to go inside the house, but now that she was there, she knew it wasn't polite to leave. She walked inside. The house smelled musty and everything seemed gray. Mrs. Novikov guided her to a small table and then she went into the kitchen to put some water on the stove for their tea.

When she came back from the kitchen, she had some beautiful teacups and saucers and a teapot to pour the tea. She sat down carefully and poured a cup of tea for herself and for Gloria. There was sugar and cream too, which they both used. Then she handed Gloria a beautifully decorated plate and asked her to arrange the cookies on it. As she placed the cookies carefully on the plate, Gloria began to feel more comfortable. She noticed that Mrs. Novikov had some photos on the wall.

"I haven't had these cookies for so many years," Mrs. Novikov said. "My mother and I used to make them together when I was a girl."

"I love to help my mama bake," Gloria said. "And I love these teacups! They are so pretty."

"They are my favorite ones," Mrs. Novikov said as she bit into a tea cake. Powdered

sugar was getting all over her fingers and her blue eyes were sparkling just like a little girl's. "You and your mama make delicious cookies."

"My mama said you were once a ballet dancer. Is that true?"

"Yes, my dear, but it was so many years ago that I can barely remember. That is why I have so many pictures on the wall. When I look at them, I can remember for just a fleeting second how it felt to be young and dance. How I loved it! But now I am so old that I am sometimes afraid to walk across the room."

Gloria thought about that for a minute. "Don't you have any children?" she asked.

"Yes. I have a son, but he has a family of his own so he doesn't have time to visit me. My wrinkles scare his tiny children. He comes once a week to bring me things to eat and that is all. My husband died ten years ago so I am alone in this house with just my memories."

They had finished eating two cookies each and Gloria asked, "May I go look at the photos?"

"Of course, my dear. Stay as long as you like."

Gloria helped clear the teacups and saucers away and then she went over to the wall of photos. Mrs. Novikov came up beside her and began to point to each photo and explain what the ballerinas were doing. She pointed herself out to Gloria.

"I can't remember looking in the mirror and seeing that young girl's face," Mrs. Novikov said wistfully.

"You look so beautiful," Gloria said.

"I was once, but now I look like Baba Yaga. I know that the children think I'm a witch, but I am just old and very wrinkled. I see that you brought a Stenovoi plat with you, but I love children and would never harm anyone. I hope you will come back and visit with me again. I feel so happy that you did."

"Yes, I will visit again. I'm not afraid," Gloria said.

"It is good to face one's fears in life," Mrs. Novikov said. "I was so afraid to perform when I was young, but I faced that fear and became a prima ballerina. It was a wonderful time in my life. I will be gone for a few minutes. Wait for me here."

Gloria waited patiently. In a few minutes, Mrs. Novikov came back. She had a beautiful doll with her. The doll was dressed in a pink tutu with pink satin toe shoes.

"I want you to have this doll. It was a gift to me from another ballerina who was my closest friend."

"Thank you, Mrs. Novikov. She's so beautiful. I will treasure her."

"I feel that she belongs with you. Come back anytime you like, and I will tell you more stories about my years as a ballerina."

Gloria smiled and Mrs. Novikov smiled back. She hugged the doll tightly as she walked home.

The End

*Every act of care plants
a little bit of magic.*

The Magic Beads

Clara and her family lived in Germany. Her grandmother lived only a few blocks away in an allotment—one of the many small garden plots known as a *kleingarten*. Living there gave her the right to grow a special garden, which connected with her neighbors' gardens to form a patchwork of greenery. Clara loved visiting because her grandmother's garden was just as magical as she was.

The garden was filled with fruit trees, vegetable beds, and flowers of every kind. Clara loved wandering through the rows of raspberries and apple trees, brushing her hands across the leaves as if the plants were greeting her. Birds trilled their morning songs from the branches, and butterflies drifted lazily in the sunlight. Hidden among the flowers were tiny gnome and fairy statues, waiting like guardians to surprise anyone who looked close enough. People came from their busy lives in Berlin to stroll through the *kleingarten*, and Clara always felt proud that her grandmother's plot was one of the most admired.

One early spring day, Clara arrived to find her grandmother kneeling in the soil, planting new seeds. The smell of damp earth and blooming hyacinths filled the air. "Clara, I'm so happy to see you!" Grandma said, pulling off her gardening gloves to hug her tightly.

"Can I help you in the garden?" Clara asked eagerly.

"Yes, of course! But let's go inside first—I have something magical to show you," Grandma replied with a twinkle in her eye.

Inside, Clara saw a small table with an assortment of treasures: fairy statues, two gnomes, a tiny stone cottage, and a saucer filled with colorful beads that sparkled in the light.

"I love the statues, and the stone cottage is perfect for fairies and gnomes," Clara said.

"A few times, I've seen something else living in one of the cottages," Grandma said with a secretive smile.

"What was it?" Clara asked eagerly.

"A little brown field mouse," Grandma answered. "It was cute, though startled when it saw me. As long as it stays outdoors, I don't mind."

"Do you have any rabbits in the garden?" Clara asked hopefully.

"I'm glad you mentioned that! There are new baby rabbits, and we'll see them before planting seeds."

"I can't wait! Could I hold one?" Clara whispered.

"We'll see. They're usually shy, but these little ones were just born. They might not be frightened yet," Grandma said kindly.

Clara pointed at the saucer. "And what are these beads for?"

"Oh, those are special. They're magical beads. My mother gave them to me. I use them when something isn't growing the way I want."

Clara thought about this carefully. She had never seen anything in Grandma's garden that wasn't thriving, perhaps the beads had quietly helped the plants all along.

After iced tea and lemon cookies, they went back outside.

"We'll need to be quiet and patient if we want the rabbits to come out," Grandma whispered, pulling soft lettuce leaves from her apron pocket.

They walked to a thicket at the garden's edge. Kneeling in the grass, Grandma laid a trail of lettuce. Clara held her breath, the air thick with anticipation.

Soon they heard rustling. The mother rabbit hopped out, twitching her nose. Her fur was the color of soft cocoa, and her ears flicked at every sound. Clara covered her mouth to hide her gasp of delight.

One by one, six tiny babies emerged. They were so small they looked like plush toys brought to life. One brave bunny hopped closer. Clara cupped a piece of lettuce in her hand, her fingers trembling. The baby sniffed, then leapt into her palm. Wide-eyed with joy, Clara met Grandma's delighted gaze. The rabbit nibbled tiny bites before hopping away to join its siblings, its little white tail bouncing like a cotton puff.

"Oh, Grandma! I'll never forget this," Clara exclaimed as they stood to head for the seed patch.

"Gardens are full of magic," Grandma said softly. "I love when butterflies land on me. Their wings are delicate and beautiful. Was the rabbit's fur soft?"

"Yes! Like a cotton ball—and its tail too," Clara laughed.

"That's why a group of bunnies is called a fluffle," Grandma said.

Clara giggled. "I love that word—fluffle!"

At the patch, Grandma had already cleared weeds. Together, they planted flower seeds in the sunny soil. Clara studied the seed packets to imagine the blossoms—tall sunflowers, bright zinnias, pink cosmos, and deep purple asters. Afterward, they watered the earth, and Clara imagined the seeds already waking beneath the soil.

Over the following weeks, Clara visited every weekend to check the sprouts. It thrilled her to see tiny green shoots pushing through the earth like little miracles. Grandma added fertilizer, while Clara watered carefully with her small tin watering can.

"How do you know how much water to give?" Clara asked one afternoon.

"I test the soil with my fingers. And sometimes I talk to the plants," Grandma said with a wink.

"Do they answer you?" Clara wondered.

"Not exactly," she replied, "but I can sense what they need."

Clara frowned. "Two of the plants aren't growing as well as the others."

"Yes, I noticed. They need magic beads," Grandma said, pulling shiny beads from her pocket that glittered like tiny jewels.

"Which ones should we use?"

Clara studied the seed packets. "Pink beads for the pink flowers, purple beads for the purple ones."

"Perfect choice," Grandma said, and together they buried the beads near the weak sprouts. Clara secretly whispered encouragement to the seeds, as if the beads could carry her words down into the soil.

Three weeks later, Clara returned to find those two plants the tallest of all, with budding flowers ready to bloom.

"Grandma! The magic beads worked!" she cried, jumping up and down.

"Are you surprised?" Grandma asked with a twinkle.

"Not exactly, but it's amazing they look even stronger than the others."

"Yes," Grandma said. "It's incredible what a little magic, sunlight, water, and care can do. Everything we want to grow must be nurtured—we can't take it for granted."

"I don't understand. What do you mean?" Clara asked.

"Every young thing—a plant, a rabbit, or a child—needs love and care to grow healthy and strong. Friendships must be nurtured too."

Clara thought for a moment, then said softly, "I think I understand now. I love you, Grandma, and I love being here with you."

"I love you too, Clara dear. These moments with you are among the happiest of my life. Now, let's see if those baby rabbits are still around. They might be bigger now."

"I'm sure they're still cute, even grown up," Clara said, hoping for another chance to feel their soft fur and to watch their little noses twitch.

As they walked back toward the thicket, the evening light cast a golden glow over the garden. Clara felt as though the whole *kleingarten* was alive, beads of magic scattered everywhere, waiting to be discovered.

The End

*Your gift may
be different,
but it matters.*

Samantha Finds Her Voice

Samantha and her family had just moved from the tiny Scottish town of Stirling to one of the biggest cities in Scotland—Edinburgh. On Monday she would be attending Sciennes Elementary School.

"Mom, I'm nervous," Samantha said. "I don't know how well I'm going to do in a class with all these big-city kids."

"I understand, dear," her mom said. "It's always a little nerve-racking to go to a new school, especially in the middle of the year. Just be yourself…you'll be fine."

"We'll see," Samantha said as her voice trailed off. She went to her room and checked her bookbag twice. Her bookbag was organized and ready, but her mind didn't feel ready. Her mom had washed and pressed her new, bright-blue uniform. It was hanging over her desk chair. Samantha wasn't sure how she felt about wearing a uniform. In her old school she could just wear her regular clothes. The one advantage would be she would be able to blend with the other students since they all had to wear uniforms too.

Her mom walked her to her new classroom and it was a good thing because Samantha felt certain that she would have gotten lost in the large building that housed the school. Her new teacher, Mrs. Dern, was kind to her and tried to help her feel welcome. After the science lesson and the math lesson, Samantha felt a bit better, but then Mrs. Dern announced something that gave her a strange, anxious feeling in her stomach. "Next week, our class will be having a talent show for the entire school. We will be performing on the auditorium stage. Tonight for your homework assignment, I want you to think about what you'd like to perform."

At the end of the school day, Samantha waited for all the other students to leave before she got up from her chair. As she passed by Mrs. Dern's desk, she asked, "Do I have to be in the talent show? Since I just got here could you excuse me? I don't really think I have any talent."

Mrs. Dern looked up from some papers she was grading and said, "Samantha, I'm sure you have talent. Do you like to draw? How about sketching or painting? Maybe you juggle? Have you ever done any magic tricks?"

Samantha shook her head no to all the questions. Then she looked down at her feet.

"Joining a class in the middle of the year is very hard, I know," Mrs. Dern said. "Think about the things you like to do. I'm sure there's something you love that you could share with the school."

Samantha walked outside and turned to look at the outside of the huge building that housed her new elementary school. It reminded her of a giant castle. She felt tiny and unimportant.

Her mom had come to pick her up. As soon as Samantha got settled into the car and they drove away, her mom asked her, "How did it go today?"

"I dunno, Mom," Samantha mumbled.

Her mom pressed her a bit. "Didn't you like your new teacher?"

"Yes, she's nice."

"Did you make any new friends?"

"Not yet. We have to perform in a talent show. I don't want to do it."

"Why not, dear? That sounds like a lot of fun."

"I don't think I have a talent and besides I'm going to get really nervous if I have to stand in front of the whole school."

The next day at recess Samantha was out in the yard when she heard a group of students from her class talking about the talent show.

"I'm going to dress up like a magician and do magic tricks," one girl said.

"I can juggle four balls in the air," one of the boys said. "I'll dress up as a clown."

"I'm going to play my guitar and sing a song I wrote," another girl said. "I'll dress up like a minstrel."

Another boy said, "I'm going to bring my paintings, my easel, and my paints and I'll paint a picture that someone requests."

Samantha listened to them, but she stood apart and didn't participate. She kept thinking and thinking but she still couldn't come up with a talent she could perform.

That night at home after they had eaten their dinner, Samantha went to her room. She picked up a stuffed toy unicorn that was one of her favorites and cuddled with it in her bedroom chair. She had been writing a story about the unicorn, but she had hidden the story in her desk drawer. She took it out and started scribbling some thoughts that she wanted to add.

Her mother knocked before she opened Samantha's door, but Samantha was so busy concentrating on writing that she hadn't heard her.

"What are you doing, dear?" her mom asked.

"I'm writing a story about a unicorn."

"Can I read it?"

"I'm almost finished with it. Then you can read it," Samantha said as she finished the sentence she was writing.

"What's it about? Can you tell me?"

"It's about a unicorn that has magical powers. She can turn into a little girl and go to school with other children."

"What a unique idea…where did you get it?"

"I'm not sure. I've been reading all about unicorns. Do you think they are real, Mom?"

"I don't know. I just know that for centuries they have been part of the history of Scotland. In fact, they are our country's national animal."

"How can the unicorn be the national animal if unicorns aren't real?"

"Who knows? There are so many unicorns in statues and paintings here in the big city that I wouldn't be at all surprised if we actually saw one someday," her mom said. "Maybe you'll have your story finished by tomorrow and then I can read it."

Samantha got up early Sunday morning. No one in their house was awake yet. She quietly worked on the unicorn story until it was finished. She read it over a couple of times. She thought to herself, *it's ready for me to share it.*

After breakfast, she shared the story with her mom. They both sat down in the living room while her mom was reading the story. Samantha watched her mom's face closely. At the beginning of the story, her mom was interested. Once in a while a smile crossed her lips as she was reading and once or twice she laughed out loud.

After her mom finished reading the story, her eyes were shining as she looked at Samantha. "Samantha, this is one of the best stories I have ever read."

Samantha was quiet for a few seconds, then she felt as if she was bursting with pride. "You really think so, Mom? After all you are my mom so you have to think it's good, right?"

Her mom giggled softly. "I can see why you might feel that way, but I promise you that I wouldn't tell you it was good if it wasn't. Samantha, I'm so proud of you. This story is amazing. I knew you loved to write, but I didn't know you could write like this. You have so much talent!"

When Samantha heard the word *talent,* she realized that she could read her story for the talent show. She was nervous about reading the story in front of the whole school, but she decided that she would practice and practice until she practically knew it by heart.

She looked through her closet to see what she could wear since it was the one day when they wouldn't have to wear their blue uniforms. She found a t-shirt with a unicorn design and a skirt that had tiny unicorns all over it. Her mom fashioned a hat with big blue eyes and a spiral horn for her to wear. She had stitched shiny sequins on it. When Samantha put it on, she felt she was a real, magical unicorn just like the girl in the story.

The day of the talent show, Samantha was the last student to perform. She had been nervous the entire day, but as soon as she got up on stage she thought about what her mom had said to her about her story. That reassurance from her mom and the beautiful unicorn hat her mom had made for her made her feel confident.

The students in her class were giggling a little bit when she started to talk but before she read her story, she pointed to the audience and said, "There might be a unicorn sitting right next to you, but if it looks like a boy or a girl how would you ever know?"

This made all the students look around at the other students who were sitting next to them. Then Samantha proceeded with telling the story about a unicorn who could change into a little girl. At night after school, the little girl would run into the forest and turn into a unicorn again. No one ever saw her change into a unicorn and back again. Her long, golden hair would turn into a sparkling, white mane.

By the middle of her story, Samantha noticed that all the students in the school were listening intently. Just like her mom, they sometimes smiled and once in a while they laughed. The magic had happened. Samantha knew what she was now. She was a storyteller, and her life would never be the same.

After she finished and said the last words, "the end," the entire auditorium of students stood up and clapped. Samantha was so proud and happy.

A few days after that, Mrs. Dern pulled her aside. "Samantha, I want to ask you for a favor."

"What is it, Mrs. Dern?" Samantha had grown to really love her teacher and would be happy to help her in any way she could.

"I volunteer at the Royal Hospital for Children and Young People," Mrs. Dern said. "There are some very sick children there. I wonder if you would come with me someday and read your story to them. I think it would bring them so much joy. If you read the unicorn story, I can buy some toy unicorns to give to them. I think both the girls and boys would love your story."

Samantha couldn't wait to accompany Mrs. Dern to the hospital. It would be difficult to see children who weren't feeling well, but if her story could bring them joy she would be excited to read it to them. She decided that she would have time to write more stories and to practice performing them. She was so thrilled that she had finally found her talent.

The End

The greatest treasures
cannot be wrapped
in boxes.

Noelle's Lost Doll

oelle was so excited. Soon it would be her birthday. Her mother had invited all of her friends to enjoy a delicious iced biscuit cake and ice cream. They would play lots of games and have fun.

On the day of the party, her friend Louisa brought a huge box with golden wrapping paper and a big red bow. Her friend Sophia brought a tiny box with a silver bow, and her friend Eveline brought a medium-sized box with polka-dotted paper and three bows—a red one, a blue one, and a yellow one.

The boxes looked so pretty that Noelle would have been happy if the boxes themselves were the actual gifts, but she still looked forward to opening them.

Her friends sang "Joyeux Anniversaire" to her, and then Noelle blew out all the candles on her cake. Noelle's mother had ordered the cake from one of the most famous bakeries in Paris—Lenôtre. The cake was in the shape of the number 8 to show her age, and it was decorated with raspberries and colorful macarons in different flavors. "Mama, the cake is so beautiful. It's almost too beautiful to eat!" Noelle exclaimed.

"We will take some pictures of it before we eat it, mon petit chou," replied Noelle's mother.

After they had each eaten two servings of cake and ice cream, Noelle went into the living room to open all her gifts. There were gifts from her mama and papa and from her grandparents. There were also gifts from aunts and uncles—some who lived nearby and others who lived far away. Last but not least were the gifts from her close friends.

She opened box after box. There were new dresses, a new hat, and new shoes from her aunts and uncles. Her grandparents had brought her stuffed toys from Disneyland Paris and tickets to take her there. Louisa had given her a huge stuffed bear that was packed so tightly in the box that when she opened it the bear's head popped out, making everyone laugh. The tiny box that her friend Sophia had brought contained a delicate gold bracelet with a heart charm. The box that Eveline had brought was filled with coloring books and crayons.

She had kept a very special box for last. It was a gift from her father—a rectangular box that Noelle hoped contained the wonderful doll she had seen in a toy shop a few months before. She knew her father had noticed her admiring it.

She slowly tore open the wrapping paper and opened the box. It was the doll she had longed for. She was so happy. She lifted the doll out of the box and hugged her tightly. Then she ran up to her father and hugged him. "Thank you, Papa! Thank you! Thank you! You knew how much I loved her."

"You're welcome, ma petite fée," her father said as he kissed Noelle's cheek.

"What will you name her?" Eveline asked.

"I don't know yet," Noelle said. "I will play with her for a  few days and then she will tell me her name." Everyone smiled, because they knew Noelle had a good imagination. She would discover the doll's name once she played with her.

"Will you bring her to our houses so that she can play with our dolls?" asked Louisa.

"Of course!" exclaimed Noelle. "We will all be great friends. I'll bring my other dolls too, just like I always do."

After her party was over, Noelle kissed her aunts, uncles, and grandparents goodbye. She hugged her friends goodbye too. Then she carried all her presents back to her room one by one. Once everything was put away, she looked at her new doll more closely. The doll looked a lot like Noelle. Her eyes and hair were the same color. When Noelle looked at her, she felt her heart grow warm with love. The doll meant even more to her because her father had bought it for her. She decided to name her Simone.

That night, before she went to sleep, she whispered to Simone, "This was the most perfect birthday ever. The only thing that would make it more perfect would be if I could fly." When she woke up the next morning, she realized she had dreamt of flying. In her dream her new doll was flying with her too. That's when she knew Simone had magical powers.

The next night she tried again. Right before sleeping, she whispered to Simone, "Today was another lovely day. The only thing that would have made it better was if I could taste my birthday cake again." And again that night she dreamt she was sitting at a table with Simone and eating a big piece of her birthday cake. Simone was truly magical.

Over the following weeks, Noelle brought Simone with her wherever she went. She packed all her dolls in a big basket and brought them to her friends' houses to play. When her mother took her to the grocery store, she brought Simone. When her father took her to the park, she took Simone. Finally the day came when her grandparents took her to Disneyland Paris. She put Simone inside a satchel and slung it over her shoulder. "Is it okay if Simone comes with us?" Noelle asked her grandmother.

Her grandmother smiled. "Of course! Simone will like the rides, I'm sure."

Noelle had so much fun that day. They went on so many rides and ate lots of delicious food. It wasn't until she got back in her grandparents' car that she realized Simone wasn't in the satchel anymore. Noelle began to cry.

"What's the matter?" her grandmother asked. "I thought we had such a wonderful day."

"We did. We did," Noelle sobbed, "but I must have dropped Simone somewhere."

"Oh dear," said her grandmother.

"Don't worry, the park will find her," her grandfather said. "I told the Lost and Found and gave them our phone number, along with the list of places we went and the rides we took."

"Thank you, Grandpa," Noelle said. She knew he was trying his best, but she felt so sad.

The next day Louisa came over. Noelle told her what had happened. Louisa said, "Noelle, I'm so sorry! I'm sure they will find her." The two friends hugged.

"I can't believe this happened," Noelle said. "I was watching her almost every minute. She was so magical. At night when I wished for something, she made it happen in my dreams."

"That's amazing," Louisa said. "I never had a magical doll before. My favorite doll is Adeline, and I'm going to leave her here to keep you company until you get Simone back."

"Are you sure?" Noelle asked.

"Yes, I'm sure," Louisa said with a smile. "You can give her back to me once Simone is found."

"Thank you, Louisa. You're such a good friend!" Noelle exclaimed.

The next day Noelle went to Sophia's house. She brought all her dolls, but of course Simone wasn't there. When she arrived, Sophia asked, "Where's Simone?"

Noelle's eyes filled with tears. "I lost her somewhere in Disneyland."

"Oh no!" Sophia exclaimed. "I know how much you love her. Maybe your papa will buy you another one."

"I don't think I would feel the same," Noelle replied. "Simone was magical. She could hear me, I think."

"Really?" Sophia asked. "Maybe I can help you find her. I still have a map of Disneyland from when my parents took me last year."

Sophia pulled a folded paper map from her desk and spread it out.

"Now…let's see. Walk me through exactly where you went and when you think you last saw her," Sophia said.

The two girls studied the map carefully. They quickly determined that Noelle had probably lost Simone somewhere on the last two rides.

"This is very helpful, Sophia. I'll give the information to my grandfather so they can check those rides at the park."

Sophia hugged Noelle before she left.

The next day Eveline came over for tea and macarons. Noelle told her what had happened.

"I'm so sorry!" Eveline said. "Once I lost my favorite stuffed bear when I was little, so I know just how you feel. We get attached to the things we love."

"Yes," Noelle said, tears welling in her eyes. "I'll never forget her."

"Don't cry, Noelle. Let's color with one of the new coloring books I brought for your birthday."

"Okay," Noelle said.

They colored and talked, and Eveline listened patiently, hugging Noelle's shoulders. "Don't lose hope," she said. "It's possible Simone might still be found."

"I don't think so. The park is so big and someone might have taken her," Noelle said. "But thank you for saying that. It makes me feel better."

That night before bed, Noelle thought about her three best friends. *I'm so lucky to have friends who care about me so much,* she thought. She drifted off to sleep and dreamt that they were all playing with their dolls—and Simone was there too. It was a beautiful dream, but when she woke up, she felt sadder than ever because Simone wasn't there.

A few days later, her grandparents arrived. Noelle loved them dearly, so she gave them each a big hug when they came inside. She noticed her grandmother was holding a bag.

"Noelle, we have a surprise for you. Look what we found!" her grandmother said, pulling Simone out of the bag.

Noelle gasped, holding out her hands. "Where did you find her?"

"She was under the back seat in our car," her grandfather said.

"How did you know?" Noelle asked.

Her grandmother smiled. "Well…it's a strange story. I had a dream about her. In the dream she told me she was under the seat and that she missed you. The next morning I checked—and there she was."

Noelle told her grandparents about the dreams she had had when Simone listened to her.

"That's incredible," her grandfather said. "It's amazing what love can do."

Noelle held Simone tightly. She thought about all the people she loved who loved her in return. She was so happy to have Simone back in her arms—and so grateful to her friends for helping her feel better when she was sad. It was wonderful to have so much love in her life.

The End

Some Freebies For You!

Visit us at **fairylandbooks.com**
to get additional resources and freebies.

We will also keep you up to date
with new offerings and updates.

Other books by Sue Elias

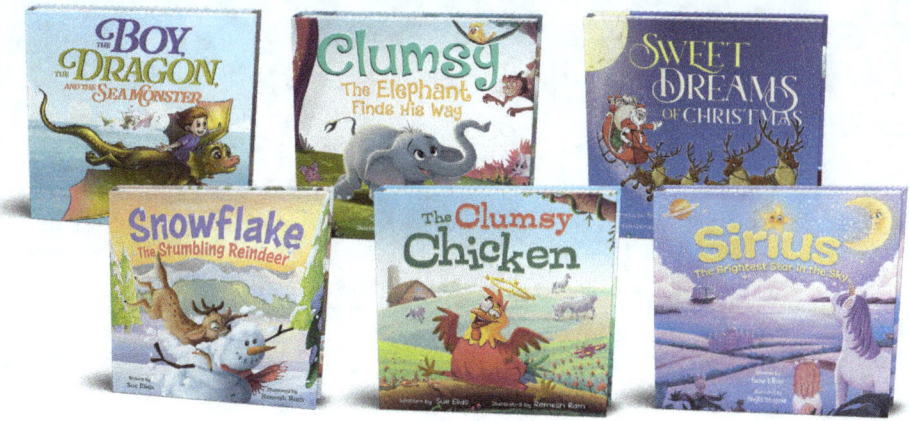